The Investor's Guide to Saudi Arabia

Opportunities in the Heart of the Middle East

Mohammad Bahareth

The Investor's Guide to Saudi Arabia:
Opportunities in the Heart of the Middle East

Mohammad Bahareth

First Edition 2025
Published by Game Changer Publishing

Paperback ISBN: 978-1-968250-78-2
Hardcover ISBN: 978-1-968250-79-9
Digital ISBN: 978-1-968250-80-5

Mohammad Bahareth
P. O. Box 126305 Jeddah 21342
Kingdom of Saudi Arabia

www.MohammadBahareth.com

Legal Disclaimer: The events and conversations in this book have been set down to the best of the author's ability, Every effort has been made to trace or contact all copyright holders. The publishers will be pleased to make good any omissions or rectify any mistakes brought to their attention at the earliest opportunity.

GC GAME CHANGER
PUBLISHING
www.GameChangerPublishing.com

READ THIS FIRST

New to Saudi Arabia?

Access clear, real-world etiquette tips
that will help you fit in, communicate
confidently, and avoid missteps.

Scan the QR Code here and
use the discount code "FREE"
to download the book free of charge:

CONTENTS

ANAS ALSUBAIHI ©

Chapter 1

Understanding the Saudi Economic Landscape Macro-Economic Indicators

GDP GROWTH RATES

Saudi Arabia, the largest economy in the Middle East and North Africa (MENA) region, has historically been characterized by its significant reliance on oil revenues. However, in recent years, the Kingdom has made concerted efforts to diversify its economy, reducing dependence on oil and promoting growth in non-oil sectors.

Recent Trends: After experiencing a contraction of 4.1% in 2020 due to the COVID-19 pandemic and a drop in oil prices, Saudi Arabia's economy rebounded strongly. In 2021, the Gross Domestic Product (GDP) grew by approximately 3.2%, bolstered by rising oil prices and a recovery in the non-oil sectors. The positive trajectory continued in 2022, with the economy expanding by an estimated 8.7%, marking the fastest growth rate in a decade.

Non-Oil Growth: Non-oil sectors have shown robust performance, contributing significantly to GDP growth. Sectors such as manufacturing, construction, and services have expanded due to government initiatives and increased private-sector participation.

INFLATION AND UNEMPLOYMENT

Inflation Rates: Inflation in Saudi Arabia has remained relatively moderate, influenced by global economic conditions and domestic policies.

Recent Data: In 2022, the inflation rate averaged around 2.5%, slightly higher than previous years, primarily due to global supply chain disruptions and increased consumer demand. The government has implemented measures to manage inflation, including subsidies and strategic reserves of essential commodities.

Unemployment Rates: Reducing unemployment is a key objective under Vision 2030, with a focus on increasing employment among Saudi nationals.

Labor Market Developments: The unemployment rate among Saudi citizens decreased to 9.7% in the first quarter of 2023, the lowest in nearly two decades. This decline is attributed to job creation in emerging sectors and reforms aimed at enhancing labor market efficiency.

Female Workforce Participation: Notably, female participation in the labor force has increased significantly, rising from 19% in 2016 to over 35% in 2023. This shift reflects broader social reforms and efforts to empower women economically.

KEY ECONOMIC SECTORS

Oil and Gas

The oil and gas sector remains a cornerstone of the Saudi economy, accounting for a substantial portion of government revenues and exports.

Saudi Aramco: As the world's largest oil-producing company, Saudi Aramco plays a pivotal role. The company's partial listing on the Saudi Stock Exchange (Tadawul) in 2019 marked a significant moment, raising capital to fund diversification projects.

Global Influence: Saudi Arabia continues to be a leading member of OPEC+, actively managing oil production levels to stabilize global oil markets.

Petrochemicals

Building on its vast hydrocarbon resources, Saudi Arabia has developed a robust petrochemical industry.

Industry Leaders: Saudi Basic Industries Corporation (SABIC), a subsidiary of Aramco since 2020, is among the world's largest petrochemical manufacturers, producing chemicals, polymers, and fertilizers.

Expansion and Innovation: The sector is focusing on technological innovation and sustainability, investing in research and development to produce advanced materials and reduce environmental impact.

NON-OIL SECTORS

Mining

Mineral Wealth: The Kingdom is endowed with rich mineral resources, including gold, phosphate, bauxite, and rare earth metals.

Sector Development: Under the Mining Investment Law of 2020, Saudi Arabia aims to attract foreign investment, streamline licensing processes, and increase the mining sector's contribution to GDP from $17 billion to $64 billion by 2030.

Tourism

Religious Tourism: Hosting Islam's two holiest cities, Mecca and Medina, Saudi Arabia is a major destination for religious pilgrims. The government is enhancing infrastructure to accommodate more visitors, aiming for 30 million Umrah pilgrims annually by 2030.

Leisure and Cultural Tourism: Significant investments are being made in projects like NEOM, the Red Sea Project, and AlUla to promote leisure tourism. The introduction of tourist visas in 2019 opened the country to international tourists, targeting 100 million visitors by 2030.

Sector Liberalization: Recent reforms have transformed the entertainment landscape. The lifting of bans on cinemas and concerts has led to a flourishing entertainment industry.

Entertainment

Sector Liberalization: Recent reforms have transformed the entertainment landscape. The lifting of bans on cinemas and concerts has led to a flourishing entertainment industry.

Economic Impact: The General Entertainment Authority (GEA) oversees the development of this sector, which is expected to contribute significantly to GDP and job creation, with projections of over 200,000 new jobs by 2030.

VISION 2030 AND ECONOMIC DIVERSIFICATION

Goals and Initiatives

Launched in 2016, Vision 2030 is Saudi Arabia's blueprint for economic transformation, aiming to diversify the economy, reduce oil dependence, and enhance public services.

Economic Diversification: The plan seeks to increase non-oil government revenue from SAR 163 billion to SAR 1 trillion and raise the share of non-oil exports in non-oil GDP from 16% to 50% by 2030.

Private Sector Growth: Encouraging private sector participation is central, with objectives to increase its contribution from 40% to 65% of GDP.

Localization: Initiatives like the National Industrial Development and Logistics Program (NIDLP) aim to localize industries such as defense, pharmaceuticals, and renewable energy.

Impact on Investment Climate

Regulatory Reforms: The government has implemented over 400 economic reforms, including the establishment of the General Authority for Foreign Trade and the Saudi Center for Commercial Arbitration, to improve the business environment.

Ease of Doing Business: Saudi Arabia has made significant strides in the World Bank's Ease of Doing Business rankings, moving up 30 places since 2018 due to improvements in starting a business, obtaining credit, and protecting minority investors.

Foreign Investment Attraction: The Kingdom has opened up sectors for foreign investment, allowing 100% foreign ownership in industries like retail, real estate, and engineering. Incentives include tax benefits, customs duty exemptions, and funding support through the Saudi Industrial Development Fund (SIDF).

Mega Projects: Ambitious projects like NEOM, a $500 billion smart city initiative, and the Qiddiya entertainment city offer vast opportunities for investors across various sectors, including technology, renewable energy, tourism, and entertainment.

Sustainability and Green Initiatives: The Saudi Green Initiative and the Middle East Green Initiative reflect the Kingdom's commitment to environmental sustainability, aiming to plant billions of trees, generate 50% of energy from renewables by 2030, and reduce carbon emissions.

ANAS ALSUBAIHI ©

KEY TAKEAWAYS

- **Economic Resilience and Growth:** Saudi Arabia has demonstrated economic resilience with strong GDP growth and a rebound from recent global challenges.

- **Diversification Efforts:** Vision 2030 is actively reshaping the economy, with significant progress in diversifying away from oil dependency.

- **Investment Opportunities:** Regulatory reforms and mega projects have created a favorable investment climate, offering numerous opportunities across various sectors.

- **Social and Cultural Transformation:** Reforms have not only economic implications but also contribute to social change, enhancing the overall quality of life and expanding the labor force.

REFERENCES

- **International Monetary Fund (IMF):** www.imf.org

- **Saudi Vision 2030:** www.vision2030.gov.sa

- **General Authority for Statistics (GaStat):** www.stats.gov.sa

- **World Bank Group:** www.worldbank.org

- **Saudi Arabian Monetary Authority (SAMA):** www.sama.gov.sa

- **Ministry of Investment (MISA):** www.misa.gov.sa

Chapter 2

Legal and Regulatory Framework

Understanding the legal and regulatory environment is crucial for any investor considering entering the Saudi Arabian market. This chapter provides an in-depth look at the laws, regulations, and procedures that govern foreign investment in the Kingdom. By familiarizing yourself with these frameworks, you can navigate the investment landscape more effectively and capitalize on the opportunities available.

FOREIGN INVESTMENT LAWS

Regulations Governing Foreign Ownership

Saudi Arabia has made significant strides in liberalizing its investment climate to attract foreign capital. The cornerstone of foreign investment regulation is the Foreign Investment Law, initially promulgated by Royal Decree No. M/1 in 2000 and subsequently amended to facilitate greater foreign participation.

- **Saudi Arabian General Investment Authority (SAGIA):** Now known as the Ministry of Investment of Saudi Arabia (MISA), this body is responsible for regulating and promoting foreign investment. It issues investment licenses, provides support services, and acts as a liaison between investors and government agencies.

- **Permitted Sectors:** Foreign investors can own up to 100% of businesses in most sectors, including retail, wholesale, industrial, and service sectors. However, certain sectors remain restricted or entirely closed to foreign investment, as listed in the Negative List issued by MISA. Restricted sectors include oil exploration and production, certain security and military activities, and real estate investment in Mecca and Medina.

- **Recent Reforms:** To enhance the investment climate, the government has reduced barriers and simplified procedures. Notable reforms include:

  - **Easing of Ownership Restrictions:** In sectors like engineering, education, and healthcare, foreign investors can now hold a majority or full ownership.

  - **Investor Protection:** Legal frameworks have been strengthened to protect foreign investors from expropriation without fair compensation and to ensure equal treatment with local investors.

Recent Reforms to Attract Foreign Investors

- **Privatization Initiatives:** Under Vision 2030, Saudi Arabia is privatizing various state-owned enterprises and opening up sectors such as water, transportation, and energy to private and foreign investment.

- **Special Economic Zones (SEZs):** The Kingdom is establishing SEZs offering tax incentives, relaxed customs regulations, and streamlined administrative procedures. Examples include the King Abdullah Economic City and the NEOM project.

- **New Companies Law:** In June 2022, Saudi Arabia introduced a new Companies Law effective from January 2023, aimed at enhancing the regulatory environment, protecting minority shareholders, and simplifying corporate procedures.

BUSINESS STRUCTURES AND ENTITIES

Choosing the right business structure is essential for compliance and operational efficiency. The most common legal entities available to foreign investors include:

Types of Legal Entities

1. Limited Liability Company (LLC)

- **Overview:** The LLC is the most common structure for foreign investors. It requires at least one shareholder and can have up to 50 shareholders.

- **Capital Requirements:** There is no minimum capital requirement unless specified by MISA for certain activities.

- **Liability:** Shareholders' liability is limited to their share in the capital.

2. Joint Stock Company (JSC)

- **Overview:** Suitable for large-scale operations, a JSC can be public or closed (private).

- **Capital Requirements:** Minimum capital of SAR 500,000 for closed JSCs and SAR 10 million for publicly listed companies.

- **Shares:** Capital is divided into transferable shares.

3. Branch of a Foreign Company

- **Overview:** Allows a foreign company to conduct business directly in Saudi Arabia without incorporating a separate legal entity.

- **Licensing:** Requires approval from MISA and registration with the Ministry of Commerce.

- **Liability:** The parent company is fully liable for the branch's obligations.

4. Technical and Scientific Office (TSO)

- **Purpose:** Established to provide technical support and facilitate communication between the parent company and local distributors or agents.

- **Restrictions:** Cannot engage in commercial activities or generate revenue.

5. Joint Ventures

- **Overview:** A contractual arrangement between a foreign investor and a Saudi partner without forming a separate legal entity.

- **Flexibility:** Terms are governed by the joint venture agreement.

Licensing Requirements

- **Investment License:** Issued by MISA, it's mandatory for foreign investors to obtain an investment license before operating.

  ○ **Application Process:** Submission of required documents, including the company's articles of association, financial statements, and a business plan.

- **Commercial Registration:** After obtaining the investment license, registration with the Ministry of Commerce is required to obtain a Commercial Registration (CR) certificate.

- **Municipal Licenses and Approvals:** Depending on the business activity, additional licenses from relevant authorities, such as the Saudi Food and Drug Authority (SFDA) for food-related businesses, may be necessary.

TAXATION AND INCENTIVES

Understanding the tax system is vital for financial planning and compliance.

Corporate Tax Rates

- **Standard Corporate Tax:** Foreign-owned entities are subject to a corporate income tax rate of 20% on taxable profits.

- **Zakat:** Saudi and GCC nationals pay Zakat, an Islamic wealth tax, at a rate of 2.5% on their net worth.

- **Withholding Tax:** This applies to payments made to non-residents, ranging from 5% to 20% depending on the nature of the payment (e.g., dividends, royalties, services).

Value Added Tax (VAT)

- **Standard Rate:** VAT is levied at a standard rate of 15% on most goods and services, increased from 5% in July 2020.

- **Registration:** Businesses with annual revenues exceeding SAR 375,000 must register for VAT with the Zakat, Tax and Customs Authority (ZATCA).

Tax Incentives for Foreign Investors

- **Tax Holidays:** Certain underdeveloped regions offer tax holidays of up to 10 years.

- **Reduced Tax Rates:** Special economic zones may provide reduced tax rates or exemptions.

- **Investment Credits:** Deductions and credits are available for activities that contribute to economic development, such as training Saudi nationals and investing in research and development.

Double Taxation Agreements (DTAs)

- **Network of Treaties:** Saudi Arabia has DTAs with over 50 countries, including major economies like China, France, India, and the United Kingdom.

- **Benefits:** DTAs prevent double taxation and may reduce withholding tax rates on cross-border payments.

INTELLECTUAL PROPERTY RIGHTS

Protecting intellectual property (IP) is essential for safeguarding your business interests.

Protection Laws

- **Legal Framework:** Saudi Arabia has a comprehensive set of laws governing IP, including patents, trademarks, copyrights, and industrial designs.

- **International Agreements:** The Kingdom is a member of the World Intellectual Property Organization (WIPO) and a signatory to key treaties like the Paris Convention and the Berne Convention.

Patents

- **Governing Body:** The Saudi Authority for Intellectual Property (SAIP) oversees patent registration.

- **Duration:** Patents are granted for 20 years from the filing date.

- **Requirements:** The invention must be new, involve an inventive step, and be industrially applicable.

Trademarks

- **Registration:** Trademarks must be registered with SAIP to gain protection.

- **Validity:** Registration is valid for 10 years and can be renewed indefinitely.

- **Enforcement:** Unauthorized use can lead to civil and criminal penalties, including fines and imprisonment.

Copyrights

- **Automatic Protection:** Literary and artistic works are automatically protected without the need for registration.

- **Duration:** Protection lasts for the life of the author plus 50 years after their death.

Industrial Designs

- **Protection:** Registered industrial designs are protected for 10 years.

Registration Processes

- **Online Portal:** SAIP provides an online platform for IP registration, making the process more efficient.

- **Documentation:** Applications typically require detailed descriptions, drawings, and proof of originality.

- **Fees:** Vary depending on the type of IP and the duration of protection sought.

Enforcement Mechanisms

- **Legal Action:** IP owners can file lawsuits against infringers in specialized commercial courts.

- **Customs Enforcement:** The Saudi Customs Authority can seize counterfeit goods at borders upon request.

COMPLIANCE AND REGULATORY CONSIDERATIONS

Anti-Money Laundering (AML) and Counter-Terrorism Financing (CTF)

- **Regulations:** Businesses must comply with AML and CTF laws, including customer due diligence and reporting suspicious transactions.

- **Enforcement:** Non-compliance can result in severe penalties, including fines and imprisonment.

Competition Law

- **Purpose:** The Competition Law prohibits anti-competitive practices such as monopolies, price-fixing, and market manipulation.

- **Authority:** The General Authority for Competition (GAC) enforces the law and reviews mergers and acquisitions for compliance.

Data Protection

- **Personal Data Protection Law (PDPL):** Implemented in 2022, the PDPL regulates the collection, processing, and storage of personal data.

- **Compliance Requirements:** Businesses must obtain consent for data processing and ensure data security.

KEY TAKEAWAYS

- Progressive Reforms: Saudi Arabia has significantly reformed its legal and regulatory frameworks to attract foreign investment, offering 100% ownership in many sectors.

- Legal Structures: Multiple business entity options are available, each with its own advantages and compliance requirements.

- Taxation: Understanding corporate tax obligations, VAT, and available incentives is crucial for financial planning.

- Intellectual Property: Robust IP laws protect investors' innovations and brands, with enforcement mechanisms to combat infringement.

- Compliance: Adhering to AML, competition, and data protection laws is essential to avoid legal pitfalls.

Note: The legal landscape in Saudi Arabia is dynamic, with ongoing reforms aimed at improving the business environment. Investors should consult legal professionals or official government sources for the most current information.

REFERENCES

- Ministry of Investment (MISA): www.misa.gov.sa

- Saudi Authority for Intellectual Property (SAIP): www.saip.gov.sa

- Zakat, Tax and Customs Authority (ZATCA): www.zatca.gov.sa

- General Authority for Competition (GAC): www.gac.gov.sa

- Ministry of Commerce: www.mc.gov.sa

- World Bank Doing Business Reports: www.worldbank.org

Chapter 3

Investment Opportunities in Key Sectors

Saudi Arabia's ambitious economic diversification under Vision 2030 has unlocked a multitude of investment opportunities across various sectors. This chapter delves into the key industries that present significant potential for foreign investors, highlighting the initiatives, projects, and regulatory changes that make the Kingdom an attractive destination for investment.

ENERGY SECTOR

Renewable Energy Initiatives

Saudi Arabia, traditionally known for its vast oil reserves, is making substantial investments in renewable energy to diversify its energy mix and meet growing domestic demand.

Saudi Green Initiative

- **Objective:** Launched in 2021, the Saudi Green Initiative aims to increase the Kingdom's reliance on clean energy and reduce carbon emissions.

- **Targets:**
  - Generate 50% of the country's energy from renewable sources by 2030.
  - Plant 10 billion trees within the Kingdom.

- **Opportunities for Investors:**
  - **Solar Energy:** With abundant sunlight, projects like the Sakaka Solar Power Plant (300 MW) have been successful, and more tenders are being issued.
  - **Wind Energy:** The Dumat Al-Jandal Wind Farm (400 MW) is the first utility-scale wind project, signaling growth potential.
  - **Hydrogen Production:** Investments in green hydrogen, such as the $5 billion NEOM Green Hydrogen Project, present cutting-edge opportunities.

Regulatory Support

Saudi Renewable Energy Project Development Office (REPDO) oversees renewable energy projects, providing transparent bidding processes.

- **Incentives:** Tax exemptions, land grants, and long-term power purchase agreements (PPAs) are offered to attract investors.

INVESTMENT IN OIL AND GAS TECHNOLOGIES

Despite the push towards renewables, oil and gas remain integral, with a focus on efficiency and technological advancement.

Upstream and Downstream Opportunities

- **Enhanced Oil Recovery (EOR):** Technologies to maximize extraction from existing fields.

- **Refining and Petrochemicals:** Expansion projects like the Jazan Refinery and integration with petrochemical complexes.

DIGITALIZATION AND INNOVATION

- **Fourth Industrial Revolution Center:** Established by Saudi Aramco to foster innovation in the energy sector.

- **Investment Areas:**

  - Artificial Intelligence (AI) and Big Data Analytics for operational efficiency.

  - Internet of Things (IoT) for real-time monitoring and predictive maintenance.

  - Cybersecurity solutions to protect critical infrastructure.

INFRASTRUCTURE AND CONSTRUCTION

Mega-Projects

Saudi Arabia is undertaking some of the world's most ambitious infrastructure projects, creating vast opportunities in construction, engineering, and related services.

NEOM City

- **Overview:** A $500 billion futuristic mega-city in the northwest, spanning 26,500 square kilometers.

- **Components:**

  - **THE LINE:** A linear city without cars or streets, powered entirely by renewable energy.

  - **OXAGON:** A floating industrial complex focusing on advanced manufacturing and research.

- **Investment Opportunities:**

  - **Construction and Engineering:** Contracts for building infrastructure, housing, and commercial spaces.

  - **Technology Integration:** Smart city solutions, AI, and robotics.

  - **Sustainability Solutions:** Renewable energy systems, water desalination, and waste management.

Red Sea Project

- **Overview:** A luxury tourism destination spread over 28,000 square kilometers along the Red Sea coast.

- **Goals:**

  - Develop 50 resorts, offering 8,000 hotel rooms and 1,300 residential properties.

  - Create an eco-friendly destination with zero waste-to-landfill policies.

- **Investment Opportunities:**

  - **Hospitality:** Hotel development and management.

  - **Infrastructure:** Airports, marinas, and transportation systems.

  - **Eco-Tourism:** Sustainable tourism activities and conservation efforts.

PUBLIC-PRIVATE PARTNERSHIPS (PPPs)

The Saudi government is leveraging PPPs to finance and operate infrastructure projects.

Sectors Open for PPPs

- **Transportation:** Roads, railways (e.g., the Haramain High-Speed Railway), and airports.

- **Utilities:** Water desalination plants and power generation.

- **Healthcare and Education:** Building and managing hospitals and schools.

Regulatory Framework

- **National Center for Privatization & PPP (NCP):** Facilitates and regulates PPP projects, offering standardized contracts and transparent bidding processes.

- **Investment Incentives:**

  - Government Guarantees: Revenue guarantees and support for land acquisition.

  - Financial Support: Access to funding from the Saudi Industrial Development Fund (SIDF) and other financial institutions.

TECHNOLOGY AND INNOVATION

Digital Transformation Initiatives

Saudi Arabia is rapidly advancing its digital infrastructure to become a global leader in technology.

Saudi Vision 2030 Digital Goals

- **E-Government:** Enhancing public services through digital platforms.

- **Digital Infrastructure:** Expanding high-speed internet coverage and 5G networks.

- **Cybersecurity:** Establishing robust systems to protect data and infrastructure.

Key Programs

- **National Digital Transformation Unit (NDU):** Coordinates digital initiatives across government entities.

- **ICT Strategy 2023:** Aims to increase the ICT sector's contribution to GDP and foster innovation.

Start-Up Ecosystem

Entrepreneurship Support

- **Monsha'at:** The Small and Medium Enterprises General Authority provides support services, funding, and regulatory assistance.

- **Wa'ed:** Saudi Aramco's entrepreneurship arm offers incubation, mentorship, and venture capital.

Innovation Hubs and Accelerators

- **King Abdullah University of Science and Technology (KAUST):** Houses a research park and innovation center.

- **MiSK Foundation:** Provides training programs, incubators, and funding for youth-led startups.

Investment Opportunities

- **FinTech:** Regulatory sandbox established by the Saudi Central Bank (SAMA) to foster innovation.

- **E-Commerce:** Rapid growth due to high internet penetration and changing consumer behavior.

- **Artificial Intelligence and Robotics:** Government initiatives to integrate AI across sectors.

HEALTHCARE AND EDUCATION

Privatization of Services

The government is opening up healthcare and education sectors to private investment to improve quality and efficiency.

Healthcare Sector

- **Saudi Health Sector Transformation Program:**

  - **Objectives:** Improve access, quality, and efficiency of healthcare services.

  - **Privatization:** Plans to privatize 295 hospitals and 2,259 primary health centers.

- **Investment Opportunities:**

  - **Hospital Management:** Operating public hospitals under private models.

  - **Medical Equipment and Supplies:** Supplying advanced medical technologies.

  - **Pharmaceuticals:** Manufacturing and research partnerships.

Opportunities in Medical Tourism

- **Strategy:** Position Saudi Arabia as a regional hub for specialized medical treatments.

- **Facilities:** Development of state-of-the-art medical cities like King Fahad Medical City.

- **Investment Areas:**

  - **Specialized Clinics:** Cardiology, oncology, and orthopedic centers.

  - **Wellness Resorts:** Combining healthcare with hospitality services.

Education Sector

- **Privatization Goals:** Increase private sector participation from 14% to 25% in K-12 education.

- **Investment Opportunities:**

  ○ **Private Schools and Universities:** Establishing institutions with international curricula.

  ○ **Educational Technology (EdTech):** Developing digital learning platforms and tools.

  ○ **Vocational Training:** Programs aligned with market needs, especially in technical fields.

TOURISM AND ENTERTAINMENT
New Tourist Visas

Visa Reforms

- **Introduction of Tourist Visas:** In 2019, Saudi Arabia launched a new visa regime allowing tourists from 49 countries to obtain visas online or on arrival.

- **Impact:**

  ○ Over 500,000 tourist visas issued in the first six months.

  ○ Boosted international interest and investment in the tourism sector.

Cultural and Entertainment Projects

Diriyah Gate Development

- **Overview:** Restoration of the UNESCO World Heritage site of At-Turaif into a cultural and lifestyle destination.

- **Investment Opportunities:**

  ○ **Hospitality:** Boutique hotels and restaurants.

  ○ **Retail:** High-end shopping experiences.

  ○ **Cultural Activities:** Museums, galleries, and cultural events.

Qiddaya Entertainment City

- **Overview:** A massive entertainment complex near Riyadh, covering 334 square kilometers.

- **Attractions:**

  ○ **Theme Parks:** Agreements with international brands for amusement parks.

  ○ **Sports Facilities:** Motor racing tracks, stadiums, and golf courses.

  ○ **Arts and Culture:** Performance venues and art installations.

- Investment Opportunities:

  ○ **Development and Construction:** Building infrastructure and facilities.

  ○ **Operational Partnerships:** Managing entertainment venues and events.

  ○ **Content Creation:** Producing local and international entertainment content.

Seasonal Events

Riyadh Season and Jeddah Season

- **Description:** Annual festivals featuring concerts, exhibitions, sports events, and cultural activities.

- **Impact:**

  ○ **Economic Boost:** Attracted millions of visitors, generating significant revenue.

- Investment Areas:
  - **Event Management:** Organizing and hosting large-scale events.
  - **Sponsorships and Marketing:** Brand partnerships and advertising.
  - **Infrastructure:** Temporary structures, stages, and facilities.

CONCLUSION

Investing in Saudi Arabia's key sectors presents a unique opportunity to participate in one of the world's most significant economic transformations. The government's commitment to diversification, coupled with ambitious projects and reforms, provides a conducive environment for investors seeking growth and innovation. By aligning with the Kingdom's strategic objectives, investors can contribute to and benefit from the nation's journey toward a diversified and sustainable economy.

ANAS ALSUBAIHI ©

KEY TAKEAWAYS

- **Diverse Opportunities: Saudi Arabia offers a wide range of investment opportunities across energy, infrastructure, technology, healthcare, education, tourism, and entertainment.**

- **Government Support: Strategic initiatives and reforms have created an investor-friendly environment with incentives and regulatory support.**

- **Growth Potential: The scale of projects and the commitment to diversification under Vision 2030 position the Kingdom as a lucrative market for long-term investment.**

REFERENCES

- **Ministry of Investment (MISA): www.misa.gov.sa**

- **Saudi Vision 2030: www.vision2030.gov.sa**

- **Saudi Green Initiative: www.greeninitiatives.gov.sa**

- **National Center for Privatization & PPP: www.ncp.gov.sa**

- **NEOM: www.neom.com**

- **Qiddiya: www.qiddiya.com**

- **Saudi Aramco: www.aramco.com**

- **Saudi Arabian General Investment Authority (SAGIA): Now MISA Monsha'at: www.monshaat.gov.sa**

- **King Abdullah Economic City: www.kaec.net**

FUTURE
INVESTMENT
INITIATIVE
من صندوق الاستثمارات العامة

Chapter 4

Financial Markets and Instruments

Saudi Arabia's financial markets have undergone significant transformation, positioning the Kingdom as a burgeoning hub for investors in the Middle East. This chapter delves into the intricacies of Saudi Arabia's financial markets, the regulatory landscape, and the unique investment instruments available, particularly in the realm of Islamic finance.

THE SAUDI STOCK EXCHANGE (TADAWUL)

Market Structure and Key Indices

Overview

The Saudi Stock Exchange, known as Tadawul, is the largest stock market in the Middle East and North Africa (MENA) region. Established in 2007, Tadawul serves as the primary platform for trading securities in Saudi Arabia, including equities, bonds, exchange-traded funds (ETFs), and derivatives.

- **Market Capitalization:** As of September 2023, Tadawul's market capitalization exceeds SAR 10 trillion (approximately USD 2.67 trillion), ranking it among the world's top exchanges.

- **Significance:** Tadawul plays a pivotal role in the Kingdom's economic diversification by facilitating capital formation and providing investment opportunities.

Market Segments

1. Main Market (TASI)

   - **Description:** The primary market where shares of large and established companies are listed.

   - **Index:** Tadawul All Share Index (TASI) tracks the performance of all companies listed on the Main Market.

2. Nomu – Parallel Market

   - **Description:** A secondary market designed for small and medium-sized enterprises (SMEs) with lighter listing requirements.

   - **Purpose:** Offers growth companies an alternative route to access capital markets.

3. Sukuk and Bonds Market

   - **Description:** Facilitates the trading of debt instruments, including Islamic bonds (sukuk) and conventional bonds.

   - **Participants:** Government entities, corporations, and financial institutions.

4. Derivatives Market

- **Description:** Launched in 2020 to provide futures contracts based on indices and single stocks.

- **Objective:** Enhances market depth and offers hedging mechanisms.

Key Indices

- **Tadawul All Share Index (TASI):** The benchmark index representing the performance of the Main Market.

- **Sector Indices:** Tadawul features 21 sector-specific indices, including Banks, Materials, Energy, and Consumer Services.

- **Nomu Index:** Tracks the performance of companies listed on the Nomu Parallel Market.

How to Trade on Tadawul

Access for Foreign Investors

Saudi Arabia has progressively opened its capital markets to foreign investors to stimulate economic growth and integration with global markets.

- **Qualified Foreign Investor (QFI) Program:**

  - **Eligibility:** Institutional investors such as banks, fund managers, and insurance companies regulated by recognized authorities.

  - **Requirements:** Minimum assets under management (AUM) of USD 500 million (subject to CMA discretion).

  - **Registration:** You must register with the Capital Market Authority (CMA) through an authorized custodian.

- **Foreign Strategic Investors (FSIs):**

  - **Description:** Allows foreign investors to acquire strategic stakes in listed companies without minimum holding periods.

  - **Objective:** Encourages long-term investment and knowledge transfer.

Trading Process

1. Account Opening:

- **Custodian Selection:** Choose a local custodian bank authorized by the CMA.

- **Documentation:** Provide necessary legal and financial documents for compliance.

2. Placing Orders:

- **Trading Hours:** Sunday to Thursday, 10:00 AM to 3:00 PM (Saudi Arabia Standard Time).

- **Order Types:** Market orders, limit orders, and special orders are available.

3. Settlement Cycle:

- **T+2 Settlement:** Transactions are settled two business days after the trade date, aligning with international practices.

4. Market Information:

- **Tadawulaty Services:** Offers investors access to real-time data, portfolio management, and corporate actions.

Investment Opportunities

- **Equities:** Shares of leading Saudi companies across various sectors.

- **Sukuk and Bonds:** Government and corporate debt instruments, including Sharia-compliant Sukuk.

- **ETFs:** Exchange-traded funds offering exposure to indices, sectors, or asset classes.

- **Derivatives:** Futures contracts for hedging or speculative purposes.

Capital Market Authority (CMA) Regulations

Compliance Requirements

The Capital Market Authority (CMA) is the regulatory body overseeing Saudi Arabia's capital markets. Established under the Capital Market Law of 2003, the CMA's mandate includes protecting investors, ensuring fairness, and promoting transparency.

Licensing and Registration

- **Authorized Persons:** Entities engaging in securities business must obtain a license from the CMA.

- **Ongoing Obligations:** Compliance with reporting, disclosure, and corporate governance standards.

Market Conduct Regulations

- **Insider Trading Prohibition:** Trading on material, non-public information is illegal.

- **Market Manipulation:** Activities that distort market prices or deceive investors are prohibited.

- **Disclosure Requirements:**

  o **Periodic Reports:** Listed companies must file quarterly and annual financial statements.

  o **Material Events:** Immediate disclosure of events affecting the company's operations or financial position.

Investor Protections

Regulatory Framework

- **Enforcement:** The CMA has the authority to investigate violations and impose sanctions, including fines and license revocations.

- **Dispute Resolution:** The Committee for the Resolution of Securities Disputes (CRSD) handles securities-related disputes.

Corporate Governance

- **Code of Corporate Governance:** Establishes principles for board responsibilities, shareholder rights, and transparency.

- **Audit Committees:** These are mandatory for listed companies to oversee financial reporting and risk management.

Anti-Money Laundering (AML) and Counter-Terrorism Financing (CTF)

- **Compliance Programs:** Firms must implement AML/CTF policies, including customer due diligence and transaction monitoring.

- **Reporting Obligations:** Suspicious activities must be reported to the Saudi Financial Intelligence Unit (SAFIU).

ISLAMIC FINANCE INSTRUMENTS

Sukuk Bonds

Overview

Sukuk are Islamic financial certificates resembling bonds but structured to comply with Shariah law. They represent ownership in tangible assets, usufructs, or services.

- **Global Standing:** Saudi Arabia is among the top issuers of sukuk worldwide.
- **Purpose:** Used to finance infrastructure projects, corporate expansions, and government expenditures.

Types of Sukuk

1. **Ijarah Sukuk:** Based on leasing contracts where the sukuk holder owns a share of the leased asset.
2. **Murabaha Sukuk:** Involves cost-plus financing agreements.
3. **Mudarabah Sukuk:** Represents a partnership where profits are shared according to a pre-agreed ratio.
4. **Istisna'a Sukuk:** Used to finance manufacturing or construction projects.

Investment Considerations

- **Shariah Compliance:** Ensures ethical investment aligning with Islamic principles.
- **Risk and Return:** Generally considered lower risk due to asset backing.
- **Liquidity:** Tradable on Tadawul's Sukuk and Bonds Market.

Shariah-Compliant Investment Funds

Overview

Shariah-compliant funds invest in assets permissible under Islamic law, avoiding prohibited activities like alcohol, gambling, and interest-based financial services.

Types of Funds

1. **Equity Funds:** Invest in Shariah-compliant stocks.
2. **Real Estate Investment Traded Funds (REITs):** Invest in income-generating real estate properties.
3. **Commodity Funds:** Engage in trading Shariah-compliant commodities.
4. **Balanced Funds:** Combine equities, sukuk, and other permissible assets.

Regulatory Oversight

- **Shariah Boards:** Funds must have a Shariah supervisory board to ensure compliance.
- **CMA Regulations:** Govern fund management, disclosure, and investor protection.

Investment Advantages

- **Ethical Investing:** Aligns with investors' moral and religious values.
- **Diversification:** Offers exposure to various asset classes and sectors.
- **Growth Potential:** Capitalizes on the expanding Islamic finance market.

KEY TAKEAWAYS

- **Evolving Financial Landscape: Saudi Arabia's financial markets are modernizing and offering diverse investment instruments.**

- **Regulatory Support: The CMA ensures a transparent and fair market environment.**

- **Accessibility for Foreign Investors: Programs like QFI facilitate foreign participation in Tadawul.**

- **Islamic Finance Opportunities: Sukuk- and Shariah-compliant funds provide unique investment avenues that align with ethical standards.**

REFERENCES

- **Saudi Stock Exchange (Tadawul): www.saudiexchange.sa**

- **Capital Market Authority (CMA): www.cma.org.sa**

- **Qualified Foreign Investor Program: CMA guidelines**

- **Islamic Financial Services Board (IFSB): www.ifsb.org**

- **Saudi Central Bank (SAMA): www.sama.gov.sa**

- **International Monetary Fund (IMF) Reports: www.imf.org**

- **Zakat, Tax and Customs Authority (ZATCA): www.zatca.gov.sa**

Chapter 5

Navigating Cultural Nuances

Understanding and respecting the cultural nuances of Saudi Arabia is essential for successful business interactions and building lasting relationships in the Kingdom. This chapter provides insights into the social and cultural norms that influence business practices, helping investors navigate the Saudi business environment with confidence and cultural sensitivity.

BUSINESS ETIQUETTE

Meeting Protocols

Scheduling Meetings

- **Advance Planning:** Schedule meetings well in advance, ideally a few weeks prior, as sudden appointments may not be well received.
- **Flexibility:** Be prepared for possible changes in schedules, as Saudis may prioritize personal commitments.
- **Prayer Times:** Consider the five daily prayer times when scheduling, as they are integral to daily life.

Punctuality

- **Arriving on Time:** Foreign visitors are expected to be punctual, even if the host may arrive later.
- **Patience:** Meetings may not start promptly; it's important to remain patient and courteous.

Greetings

- **Handshakes:** A traditional greeting involves a handshake with the right hand. Handshakes may be accompanied by placing the left hand over the heart.
- **Respectful Address:** Use appropriate titles and full names when addressing counterparts, such as "Sheikh," "Doctor," or "Mr./Mrs."

Exchange of Business Cards

- **Presentation:** Offer and receive business cards with the right hand or both hands.
- **Language:** Having one side of your business card translated into Arabic is appreciated.

Communication Styles

Language

- **Arabic:** The official language is Arabic. While English is widely used in business, having materials in Arabic demonstrates respect.
- **Interpreters:** Consider hiring professional interpreters for important meetings to ensure clear communication.

Communication Approach

- **Indirect Communication:** Saudis often communicate in a nuanced and indirect manner to maintain harmony and avoid conflict.
- **Contextual Understanding:** Pay attention to non-verbal cues, tone of voice, and context.
- **Politeness and Respect:** Avoid confrontational language; express disagreements diplomatically.

Building Rapport

- **Personal Connections:** Invest time in getting to know your counterparts personally before discussing business matters.
- **Small Talk:** Engage in conversations about family, culture, and general interests to build rapport.

CULTURAL SENSITIVITIES

Religious Considerations

Islamic Practices

- **Prayer Times:** Muslims pray five times a day. Meetings may pause for prayer; showing understanding is important.
- **Ramadan:** During the holy month of Ramadan, Muslims fast from dawn to sunset.
  - o **Business Hours:** Working hours may be reduced.
  - o **Etiquette:** Avoid eating, drinking, or smoking in public during fasting hours.

Dress Code

- **Modest Attire:** Dress conservatively to respect cultural norms.
  - o **Men:** Suits or long-sleeved shirts and trousers.
  - o **Women:** Professional attire covering arms and legs; wearing an abaya (a loose-fitting black cloak) and headscarf in public spaces is advisable.

Gender Dynamics in Business

Evolving Norms

- **Increased Participation:** Women's participation in the workforce has significantly increased due to recent reforms.
- **Professional Interactions:** Mixed-gender workplaces are becoming more common, especially in urban areas.

Etiquette

- **Greetings:** Physical contact between unrelated men and women is generally avoided.
  - o **Men:** Wait for a female counterpart to extend her hand first. If she does not, a polite nod and verbal greeting suffice.
- **Respectful Communication:** Maintain professionalism and avoid personal topics unless initiated.

Social Customs

Hospitality

- **Generosity:** Hospitality is a cornerstone of Saudi culture.

- **Refreshments:** Accept offers of coffee (gahwa), tea, or dates as a sign of goodwill.

Gift Giving

- **Appropriateness:** Gifts are not mandatory but appreciated. Avoid overly expensive items.
- **Presentation:** Offer gifts with the right hand or both hands. Avoid gifts that may conflict with Islamic values (e.g., alcohol, pork products).

BUILDING RELATIONSHIPS

Importance of Trust and Personal Connections

Relationship-Oriented Culture

- **Trust Building:** Establishing personal trust is crucial before entering business agreements.
- **Long-Term Commitment:** Demonstrating a commitment to a long-term relationship fosters confidence.

Social Interactions

- **Networking Events:** Attend social gatherings and events when invited.
- **Family Values:** Showing respect for family and understanding its importance strengthens bonds.

Networking Strategies

Utilizing Local Contacts

- **Introductions:** Being introduced by a mutual acquaintance or a respected local figure can facilitate connections.

- **Advisors and Consultants:** Engage local advisors who understand the cultural and business landscape.

Participation in Business Forums

- **Chambers of Commerce:** Join organizations like the Council of Saudi Chambers to network with local businesses.
- **Trade Missions:** Participate in trade delegations and investment forums to expand your network.

Understanding Hierarchies and Decision-Making

Organizational Structures

- **Hierarchy:** Saudi businesses often have hierarchical structures with clear lines of authority.
- **Decision Makers:** Key decisions are typically made by top executives or family heads in family-owned businesses.

Meeting with Decision Makers

- **Access:** It may take time to reach senior decision-makers; be patient and respectful during the process.
- **Presentations:** Tailor presentations to address the interests of senior leaders.

Negotiation Tactics

Negotiation Style

- **Patience:** Negotiations may be prolonged; rushing is considered disrespectful.
- **Flexibility:** Be prepared to adapt your proposals based on feedback.
- **Win-Win Approach:** Emphasize mutual benefits and long-term cooperation.

Agreements

- **Verbal Commitments:** Oral agreements are valued but should be followed up with written contracts.

- **Contracts:** Ensure contracts are clear, detailed, and translated into Arabic.

Cultural Do's and Don'ts

Do's

- **Respect Religion and Customs:** Show respect for Islamic practices and cultural norms.

- **Learn Basic Arabic Phrases:** Using greetings and expressions in Arabic is appreciated.

- **Demonstrate Patience:** Show willingness to invest time in building relationships.

Don'ts

- **Avoid Sensitive Topics:** Refrain from discussing politics, religion, or regional conflicts unless initiated.

- **No Public Displays of Affection:** Such behavior is considered inappropriate in public spaces.

- **Do Not Use the Left Hand:** Avoid using the left hand when offering items or eating, as it is considered unclean.

Adapting to the Saudi Business Environment

Cultural Intelligence

- **Awareness:** Educate yourself about Saudi history, culture, and societal changes.

- **Open-Mindedness:** Approach cultural differences with respect and a willingness to learn.

Professional Support

- **Cultural Training:** Consider cultural competency training for yourself and your team.

- **Local Partnerships:** Collaborate with local businesses to gain insights and enhance credibility.

Case Study: Successful Cross-Cultural Engagement

Background

An international technology firm sought to enter the Saudi market by partnering with a local company to provide cybersecurity solutions.

Approach

- **Cultural Preparation:** The firm invested in cultural training for its executives.

- **Building Trust:** They dedicated time to develop personal relationships with Saudi counterparts through multiple visits and social engagements.

- **Respecting Protocols:** Adhered to local customs during meetings, including dress code and greeting etiquette.

- **Communication:** Utilized professional interpreters and ensured all materials were available in Arabic.

Outcome

- **Successful Partnership:** Established a joint venture that benefited from combined expertise.

- **Market Acceptance:** Gained trust and credibility in the local market, leading to further opportunities.

ANAS ALSUBAIHI ©

CONCLUSION

Navigating the cultural nuances of Saudi Arabia is not merely about avoiding faux pas; it's about embracing a different way of doing business that values relationships, respect, and mutual understanding. By investing time and effort into understanding these cultural dynamics, investors can build strong partnerships and achieve sustainable success in the Kingdom.

Note: Cultural norms can vary between regions and evolve over time. It's advisable to seek current, region-specific guidance and remain adaptable to local practices.

KEY TAKEAWAYS

- **Cultural Sensitivity is Crucial:** Respecting and adapting to Saudi cultural norms facilitates successful business relationships.

- **Invest in Relationships:** Personal connections and trust are foundational to business dealings in Saudi Arabia.

- **Prepare Thoroughly:** Understanding social and business etiquette reduces misunderstandings and fosters positive interactions.

- **Be Patient and Respectful:** Patience in negotiations and respect for hierarchical structures enhance partnership prospects.

REFERENCES

- **Saudi Customs and Etiquette:** Saudi Tourism Authority

- **Cultural Intelligence for Global Executives: Harvard Business Review articles on cultural competence**

- **The Ministry of Culture:** www.moc.gov.sa

- **Council of Saudi Chambers:** www.csc.org.sa

Chapter 6

Risk Management and Compliance

Investing in any foreign market carries inherent risks, and Saudi Arabia is no exception. While the Kingdom offers numerous opportunities, it is essential for investors to understand and manage potential risks to safeguard their investments. This chapter explores the various political, economic, legal, and compliance risks associated with investing in Saudi Arabia and provides strategies to mitigate them.

POLITICAL AND ECONOMIC RISKS

Regional Geopolitics

Overview

Saudi Arabia is situated in a geopolitically sensitive region, sharing borders with countries experiencing political instability and conflict. Regional tensions can impact the Kingdom's security, economy, and investment climate.

Key Considerations

- **Regional Conflicts:** Proximity to conflict zones such as Yemen can pose security risks, including potential attacks on infrastructure.

- **Diplomatic Relations:** Fluctuations in relationships with neighboring countries and global powers can affect trade and investment.

- **Policy Shifts:** Geopolitical developments may lead to sudden changes in government policies, impacting sectors like energy, defense, and foreign investment.

Risk Mitigation Strategies

- **Stay Informed:** Regularly monitor regional news and government advisories.

- **Political Risk Insurance:** Consider obtaining insurance to protect against losses from political events.

- **Diversification:** Spread investments across different sectors and regions within Saudi Arabia to minimize exposure.

Oil Price Volatility

Impact on the Economy

As one of the world's leading oil producers, Saudi Arabia's economy is significantly influenced by global oil prices. Fluctuations can affect government revenues, spending, and economic growth.

Key Considerations

- **Government Spending:** High dependency on oil revenues means that price drops can lead to reduced government spending on projects and subsidies.

- **Currency Stability:** The Saudi Riyal is pegged to the US Dollar, but prolonged low oil prices could pressure this arrangement.

- **Sectoral Impact:** Sectors reliant on government contracts may face delays or cancellations during periods of low oil prices.

Risk Mitigation Strategies

- **Hedging:** Use financial instruments to hedge against commodity price fluctuations.

- **Non-Oil Sector Focus:** Invest in sectors less affected by oil prices, such as technology, healthcare, and education.

- **Long-Term Perspective:** Recognize that while oil prices may fluctuate, Saudi Arabia's commitment to diversification under Vision 2030 aims to reduce economic dependency on oil.

LEGAL RISKS

Contract Enforcement

Legal Framework

Saudi Arabia has been reforming its legal system to enhance the business environment, but differences in legal practices compared to other jurisdictions can pose challenges.

Key Considerations

- **Sharia Law Influence:** The legal system is based on Islamic law (Sharia), which may differ from common law or civil law principles.

- **Contract Interpretation:** Courts may interpret contractual terms differently, emphasizing fairness and intention over strict literal meanings.

- **Language:** Arabic is the official language for legal documents and court proceedings; translations may lead to discrepancies.

Risk Mitigation Strategies

- **Legal Counsel:** Engage reputable local legal firms with expertise in both Saudi and international law.

- **Clear Contracts:** Draft contracts with precise terms, including dispute resolution clauses specifying governing law and jurisdiction.

- **Bilingual Documentation:** Ensure contracts are accurately translated and reviewed in both English and Arabic.

Dispute Resolution Mechanisms

Options for Investors

- **Saudi Courts:** The traditional route, but proceedings may be lengthy and outcomes uncertain due to legal system differences.

- **Arbitration:** Increasingly favored for resolving commercial disputes.

Arbitration Centers

- **Saudi Center for Commercial Arbitration (SCCA):**

  - **Establishment:** Founded in 2014 to provide alternative dispute resolution services.

  - **Services:** Offers arbitration and mediation with rules based on international standards.

  - **Language Flexibility:** Proceedings can be conducted in English or Arabic.

International Arbitration

- **New York Convention:** Saudi Arabia is a signatory, allowing for the recognition and enforcement of foreign arbitral awards.

- **Choice of Venue:** Parties may agree to arbitrate in neutral locations, though enforcement of foreign judgments may face challenges.

Risk Mitigation Strategies

- **Include Arbitration Clauses:** Specify arbitration as the preferred dispute resolution method in contracts.

- **Select Governing Law:** Clearly state the applicable law and jurisdiction.

- **Due Diligence:** Assess the dispute resolution mechanisms preferred in your industry and by your partners.

COMPLIANCE WITH INTERNATIONAL STANDARDS

Anti-Money Laundering (AML)

Regulatory Framework

Saudi Arabia has implemented robust AML laws in line with international standards to prevent illicit financial activities.

- **Legal Basis:** The Anti-Money Laundering Law issued by Royal Decree M/20 in 2017.

- **Regulatory Bodies:**

  - **Saudi Central Bank (SAMA):** Oversees financial institutions.

  - **Capital Market Authority (CMA):** Regulates capital markets and securities firms.

  - **Saudi Financial Intelligence Unit (SAFIU):** Responsible for receiving and analyzing suspicious transaction reports.

Key Requirements

- **Customer Due Diligence (CDD):** Verify the identity of clients and beneficial owners.

- **Record Keeping:** Maintain transaction records for at least ten years.

- **Reporting Obligations:** Report suspicious transactions to SAFIU promptly.

- **Training:** Regular staff training on AML policies and procedures.

Penalties for Non-Compliance

- **Fines:** Up to SAR 5 million (approximately USD 1.33 million).

- **Imprisonment:** For individuals involved in money laundering activities.

- **Reputational Damage:** Negative impact on the firm's credibility and business relationships.

Risk Mitigation Strategies

- **Implement AML Policies:** Develop comprehensive internal policies aligned with legal requirements.

- **Regular Audits:** Conduct periodic compliance audits and risk assessments.

- **Employee Training:** Ensure staff are knowledgeable about AML obligations.

Counter-Terrorism Financing (CTF)

Regulatory Framework

Saudi Arabia actively combats terrorism financing, aligning its regulations with global efforts.

- **Legal Basis:** The Law of Combating Crimes of Terrorism and Its Financing issued in 2017.
- **International Cooperation:** Member of the Financial Action Task Force (FATF) since 2019.

Key Requirements

- **Sanctions Compliance:** Screen clients and transactions against national and international sanctions lists.
- **Enhanced Due Diligence:** For high-risk customers and transactions.
- **Reporting:** Mandatory reporting of suspected terrorism financing activities.

Risk Mitigation Strategies

- **Screening Systems:** Implement technology solutions to monitor and screen transactions.
- **Risk Assessment:** Identify and assess potential CTF risks in business operations.
- **Policy Integration:** Incorporate CTF measures into overall compliance programs.

OPERATIONAL RISKS

Supply Chain Risks

Considerations

- **Logistics Challenges:** Potential delays due to customs procedures or infrastructure limitations.
- **Vendor Reliability:** Dependence on local suppliers may pose quality or reliability issues.

Risk Mitigation Strategies

- **Due Diligence:** Vet suppliers and partners thoroughly.
- **Diversification:** Avoid reliance on a single supplier or logistic route.
- **Contracts:** Include clauses addressing performance standards and remedies.

Cybersecurity Risks

Considerations

- **Increasing Threats:** Rising cyberattacks targeting businesses in the region.
- **Data Protection Laws:** Compliance with the Personal Data Protection Law (PDPL) enacted in 2021.

Risk Mitigation Strategies

- **Security Measures:** Implement robust cybersecurity protocols.
- **Staff Training:** Educate employees on cyber risks and safe practices.
- **Incident Response Plan:** Develop a plan to respond to and recover from cyber incidents.

REPUTATIONAL RISKS

Social Responsibility and Ethics

Considerations

- **Cultural Sensitivity:** Misunderstandings or insensitivity can harm a company's reputation.
- **Environmental Impact:** Non-compliance with environmental regulations can lead to penalties and public backlash.

Risk Mitigation Strategies

- **Corporate Social Responsibility (CSR):** Engage in initiatives that benefit the local community.
- **Compliance:** Adhere strictly to environmental and social regulations.
- **Transparency:** Maintain open communication with stakeholders.

REGULATORY CHANGES

Dynamic Regulatory Environment

Considerations

- **Reforms:** Ongoing legal and regulatory reforms may impact business operations.
- **Compliance Updates:** New laws may require changes in compliance practices.

Risk Mitigation Strategies

- **Continuous Monitoring:** Keep abreast of regulatory developments.
- **Legal Counsel:** Maintain relationships with local legal experts.
- **Adaptability:** Be prepared to adjust business practices in response to new regulations.

Strategies for Effective Risk Management

Comprehensive Risk Assessment

- **Identify Risks:** Conduct thorough analyses to identify all potential risks.
- **Prioritize:** Assess the likelihood and impact to prioritize risk management efforts.
- **Mitigation Plans:** Develop strategies to address each identified risk.

Insurance Solutions

- **Types of Insurance:**
  - **Political Risk Insurance:** Covers losses from political events.
  - **Trade Credit Insurance:** Protects against non-payment by customers.

- ○ **Property and Casualty Insurance:** Covers physical assets and liability risks.

Local Partnerships

- **Benefits:** Local partners can provide insights into market dynamics and help navigate regulatory environments.

- **Selection:** Choose partners with strong reputations and aligned business values.

Corporate Governance

- **Best Practices:** Implement strong governance structures to ensure accountability and compliance.

- **Board Composition:** Include members with expertise in risk management and local laws.

CONCLUSION

Risk management and compliance are integral components of a successful investment strategy in Saudi Arabia. By understanding the multifaceted risks and implementing robust mitigation strategies, investors can navigate the complexities of the Saudi market effectively. Embracing a proactive approach to risk ensures not only the protection of assets but also contributes to sustainable business growth in the Kingdom.

Note: The information provided in this chapter is for general guidance only and should not be considered legal or financial advice. Investors are encouraged to consult with professional advisors to address specific risk management and compliance needs.

KEY TAKEAWAYS

- Proactive Risk Management: Identifying and addressing risks before they materialize protects investments.

- Legal Compliance: Adhering to local and international laws is essential to avoid penalties and reputational damage.

- Cultural Understanding: Respecting local customs and business practices enhances relationships and mitigates social risks.

- Continuous Monitoring: Stay informed about geopolitical developments and regulatory changes to adapt strategies accordingly.

REFERENCES

- Ministry of Investment (MISA): www.misa.gov.sa

- Saudi Central Bank (SAMA): www.sama.gov.sa

- Capital Market Authority (CMA): www.cma.org.sa

- Saudi Center for Commercial Arbitration (SCCA): www.sadr.org

- Financial Action Task Force (FATF): www.fatf-gafi.org

- Anti-Money Laundering Law: Royal Decree M/20, 2017.

- Law of Combating Crimes of Terrorism and Its Financing: Royal Decree No. M/21, 2017.

- Personal Data Protection Law (PDPL): Issued in 2021 by the Saudi Data & AI Authority (SDAIA).

Chapter 7

Practical Steps to Investing

Embarking on an investment journey in Saudi Arabia requires a clear understanding of the practical steps involved. This chapter provides a comprehensive guide on market entry strategies, the process of setting up a business, understanding labor laws, and navigating the banking and financial services sector. By following these guidelines, investors can establish a solid foundation for their ventures in the Kingdom.

MARKET ENTRY STRATEGIES

Choosing the right market entry strategy is crucial for aligning your business objectives with the regulatory environment and market dynamics of Saudi Arabia.

Joint Ventures

Overview

A joint venture (JV) involves partnering with a local Saudi entity to establish a new business. This strategy combines the foreign investor's expertise and capital with the local partner's market knowledge and networks.

Types of Joint Ventures

- **Contractual Joint Ventures:** An agreement between parties without forming a new legal entity.
- **Equity Joint Ventures:** Establishing a new company where ownership and profits are shared according to the equity contributions.

Benefits

- **Local Expertise:** Access to the local partner's understanding of the market, culture, and regulatory landscape.
- **Shared Risk:** Distribution of financial and operational risks.
- **Market Access:** Facilitates entry into sectors where foreign ownership is restricted or where local partnership is advantageous.

Considerations

- **Partner Selection:** Conduct thorough due diligence to ensure alignment of business goals and values.
- **Legal Agreements:** Clearly define roles, responsibilities, profit-sharing, and dispute resolution mechanisms.
- **Control and Management:** Establish governance structures to manage decision-making processes.

Wholly Foreign-Owned Enterprises

Overview

Saudi Arabia allows foreign investors to establish companies with 100% foreign ownership in many sectors, reflecting the Kingdom's commitment to attracting international investment.

Types of Entities

- **Limited Liability Company (LLC):** The most common structure for wholly foreign-owned businesses.

- **Branch Office:** Extension of a foreign parent company, engaging in activities similar to the parent.

- **Technical and Scientific Office (TSO):** For companies aiming to provide technical support without commercial activities.

Benefits

- **Full Control:** Complete ownership and control over business operations and decision-making.

- **Profit Retention:** No obligation to share profits with local partners.

- **Brand Protection:** Greater ability to maintain brand integrity and corporate culture.

Considerations

- **Sector Restrictions:** Ensure the intended business activity is permitted for 100% foreign ownership.

- **Capital Requirements:** Be aware of any minimum capital requirements specified by the Ministry of Investment (MISA).

- **Regulatory Compliance:** Adherence to Saudi laws and regulations without reliance on a local partner's expertise.

Setting Up a Business

Establishing a business in Saudi Arabia involves several steps, from obtaining the necessary licenses to registering with relevant authorities. The process has been streamlined in recent years to facilitate foreign investment.

Step-by-Step Guide

1. Obtain an Investment License from MISA

   - **Application Submission:** Provide required documents, including:

     ○ Company profile and audited financial statements.

     ○ Business plan detailing the intended activities.

     ○ Copies of the company's articles of association and commercial registration.

   - **Approval Timeframe:** Typically within 5-10 business days if all documents are in order.

2. Register the Company with the Ministry of Commerce

   - **Company Name Reservation:** Reserve a unique company name in Arabic.

   - **Articles of Association (AoA):** Draft and notarize the AoA in Arabic.

   - **Commercial Registration (CR):** Obtain the CR certificate, which serves as the company's ID.

3. Open a Bank Account

   - **Capital Deposit:** Deposit the initial capital in a Saudi bank account.

   - **Bank Certificate:** Obtain a certificate confirming the capital deposit.

4. Register with the Chamber of Commerce

- **Membership:** Mandatory for all companies to join the local Chamber of Commerce.

- **Benefits:** Access to networking events, resources, and support services.

5. Obtain Municipal Licenses

- **Premises Approval:** Secure licenses for the physical location of the business.

- **Inspections:** Comply with health, safety, and zoning regulations.

6. Register for Taxes

- **Zakat, Tax and Customs Authority (ZATCA):** Register for corporate income tax and VAT.

- **Tax Identification Number (TIN):** Obtain a TIN for tax filing purposes.

7. Register with the General Organization for Social Insurance (GOSI)

- **Employee Registration:** Mandatory for companies hiring employees.

- **Contributions:** Both employers and employees contribute to social insurance schemes.

8. Obtain Work Visas and Residency Permits (Iqama)

- **Sponsorship:** The company acts as a sponsor for foreign employees.

- **Visas:** Apply for work visas through the Ministry of Human Resources and Social Development (MHRSD).

Required Documentation

- For MISA License:

  o Application form.

  o Feasibility study or business plan.

  o Copies of passports for foreign shareholders.

  o Financial statements of the parent company (if applicable).

- For Company Registration:

  o Notarized Articles of Association.

  o Capital deposit certificate.

  o Proof of registered office address.

- For Municipal Licenses:

  o Lease agreement or property ownership documents.

  o Compliance certificates for health and safety.

HIRING AND LABOR LAWS

Understanding Saudi labor laws is crucial for compliance and effective workforce management.

Saudization Policies (Nitaqat Program)

Overview

The Nitaqat program mandates that companies employ a certain percentage of Saudi nationals, with quotas varying by industry and company size.

Key Points

- **Categorization:** Companies are classified into bands (Platinum, Green, Yellow, Red) based on their Saudization rates.

- **Compliance:** Higher compliance results in benefits such as easier visa processing, while non-compliance can lead to restrictions.

- **Exemptions:** Certain sectors and professions may have specific guidelines.

Strategies for Compliance

- **Recruitment:** Prioritize hiring qualified Saudi nationals.

- **Training Programs:** Invest in training and development to build local talent.

- **Outsourcing:** For non-core activities, consider outsourcing to firms compliant with Saudization.

Work Visas and Permits

Employment of Foreign Nationals

- **Sponsorship System:** Employers sponsor foreign employees and are responsible for their legal status.

- **Work Visas:** Issued for specific job roles, requiring documentation such as employment contracts and academic qualifications.

- **Residency Permits (Iqama):** Allows the employee to live and work in Saudi Arabia, renewable annually.

Application Process

1. **Work Visa Authorization:** Obtain approval from MHRSD.

2. **Visa Issuance:** Processed through the Saudi embassy or consulate in the employee's home country.

3. **Medical Examination:** Required health checks before and after arrival.

4. **Iqama Application:** Submit to the General Directorate of Passports (Jawazat) upon arrival.

Compliance Requirements

- **Employment Contracts:** Must be written in Arabic, outlining terms and conditions.

- **Labor Law Adherence:** Comply with regulations on working hours, leave entitlements, and termination procedures.

- **Record Keeping:** Maintain accurate records of employees' work permits and visas.

BANKING AND FINANCIAL SERVICES

Access to banking services is essential for business operations, including transactions, financing, and payroll management.

Opening Corporate Bank Accounts

Requirements

- **Company Documentation:**

  o Commercial Registration Certificate.

  o Articles of Association.

  o MISA Investment License.

  o Identification documents of authorized signatories.

- **Account Types:**
  - o **Current Accounts:** For daily transactions and payments.
  - o **Savings Accounts:** For surplus funds with interest earnings (note that conventional interest may conflict with Islamic principles; Shariah-compliant options are available).

Process

1. **Bank Selection:** Choose a bank that offers services aligned with your business needs, considering factors like branch network, online banking, and language support.

2. **Application Submission:** Provide the required documents and complete the bank's account opening forms.

3. **Compliance Checks:** Banks will conduct due diligence, including AML and KYC procedures.

4. **Account Activation:** Upon approval, the account is activated for transactions.

Accessing Credit and Financing

Financing Options

- **Commercial Banks:** Offer loans, credit facilities, and trade finance solutions.
- **Saudi Industrial Development Fund (SIDF):**
  - o **Purpose:** Provides medium to long-term loans to industrial projects.
  - o **Eligibility:** Projects that contribute to the development of the industrial sector.

- **Saudi Arabian Monetary Authority (SAMA) Programs:**
  - o **SME Financing:** Initiatives to support small and medium-sized enterprises.
  - o **Export Financing:** Facilities to promote non-oil exports.

- **Venture Capital and Private Equity:**
  - o **Investment Firms:** Provide equity financing to startups and growth-stage companies.
  - o **Government Funds:** Entities like the Public Investment Fund (PIF) invest in strategic sectors.

Shariah-Compliant Financing

- **Islamic Banking:** Financial products that comply with Islamic law, avoiding interest-based transactions.
- **Common Instruments:**
  - o **Murabaha:** Cost-plus financing for asset purchases.
  - o **Mudarabah:** Profit-sharing arrangements.
  - o **Ijara:** Lease financing agreements.

Application Process for Financing

1. **Prepare a Business Plan:** Demonstrate the project's feasibility and financial projections.

2. **Submit Documentation:** Include financial statements, corporate documents, and collateral details.

3. **Credit Evaluation:** The lender assesses creditworthiness and risk.

4. **Negotiation of Terms:** Discuss interest rates (profit rates for Islamic financing), repayment schedules, and covenants.

5. **Legal Documentation:** Finalize agreements with the assistance of legal counsel.

Navigating Government Services

E-Government Platforms

Saudi Arabia has implemented several online platforms to streamline business processes.

- **MISA eServices:** For investment license applications and renewals.

- **Ministry of Commerce:** Online company registration and name reservation.

- **Qiwa Platform:** Managed by MHRSD for labor-related services, including work visas and Saudization compliance.

- **Absher:** For individual services, including visa renewals and traffic violations.

Support Services

- **Investor Service Centers:** MISA provides dedicated centers offering guidance and support to investors.

Case Study: Setting Up a Manufacturing Plant

Background

An international manufacturing company aims to establish a production facility in Saudi Arabia to serve the Middle East market.

Approach

1. Market Entry Strategy:

- Opted for a wholly foreign-owned LLC to maintain control over operations.

- Chose a location in an industrial city with incentives.

2. Business Setup:

- Obtained an investment license from MISA.

- Registered the company and secured necessary municipal licenses.

3. Compliance with Saudization:

- Developed a recruitment plan to hire and train Saudi nationals.

- Collaborated with technical colleges for workforce development.

4. Financing:

- Secured a loan from the SIDF with favorable terms.

- Accessed export financing for regional distribution.

5. Banking Services:

- Opened accounts with a local bank offering Islamic financing options.

- Utilized online platforms for efficient transaction management.

Outcome

- **Successful Launch:** Began production within projected timelines.

- **Regulatory Compliance:** Met all legal requirements, avoiding delays.

- **Local Integration:** Established strong relationships with government entities and the local community.

- **One-Stop Shops:** Facilitate interactions with multiple government agencies in one location.

Key Considerations for Successful Setup

- **Legal Compliance:** Adhere strictly to laws and regulations to avoid penalties.

- **Cultural Sensitivity:** Respect local customs and business practices.

- **Professional Advice:** Engage local consultants, lawyers, and accountants.

- **Networking:** Build relationships with local businesses and authorities.

CONCLUSION

Setting up a business in Saudi Arabia involves navigating a well-defined process that has been increasingly optimized for foreign investors. By understanding the practical steps and leveraging available resources, investors can establish their operations effectively. The Kingdom's commitment to economic diversification and regulatory reforms presents a conducive environment for businesses to thrive.

Note: This chapter provides general guidance on setting up a business in Saudi Arabia. Regulations and procedures may change, so it is advisable to consult with professional advisors and official government sources for the most current information.

KEY TAKEAWAYS

- **Strategic Planning:** Selecting the appropriate market entry strategy aligns your business with legal and operational needs.

- **Regulatory Adherence:** Compliance with setup procedures and labor laws is critical for smooth operations.

- **Resource Utilization:** Leveraging government services and financial institutions enhances efficiency and access to capital.

- **Cultural Integration:** Embracing local practices and investing in the workforce contributes to sustainable success.

REFERENCES

- **Ministry of Investment (MISA):** www.misa.gov.sa

- **Ministry of Commerce:** www.mc.gov.sa

- **Ministry of Human Resources and Social Development (MHRSD):** www.hrsd.gov.sa

- **General Organization for Social Insurance (GOSI):** www.gosi.gov.sa

- **Zakat, Tax and Customs Authority (ZATCA):** www.zatca.gov.sa

- **Saudi Industrial Development Fund (SIDF):** www.sidf.gov.sa

- **Saudi Central Bank (SAMA):** www.sama.gov.sa

Chapter 8

Case Studies and Success Stories

Understanding real-world examples of how businesses have successfully invested in Saudi Arabia provides valuable insights into effective strategies, challenges overcome, and lessons learned. This chapter presents case studies of multinational corporations, successful startups, and notable projects that have thrived in the Saudi market. These examples illustrate the practical application of concepts discussed in previous chapters and highlight opportunities for potential investors.

MULTINATIONAL CORPORATIONS IN SAUDI ARABIA

Case Study 1: General Electric (GE)

Background

General Electric (GE), a global leader in energy, healthcare, and aviation, has been operating in Saudi Arabia for over 80 years. GE's long-standing presence showcases its commitment to the Kingdom's development and its ability to adapt to the evolving business landscape.

Strategies and Outcomes

- **Localization Initiatives:**

  o **GE Manufacturing and Technology Center (GEMTEC):** Established in Dammam in 2011, GEMTEC serves as a manufacturing hub for advanced gas turbines and provides services across the Middle East.

  o **Job Creation:** GEMTEC employs over 500 professionals, with a significant proportion of Saudi nationals, contributing to Saudization efforts.

  o **Training Programs:** GE has partnered with local universities to offer training and development programs, enhancing the skills of the local workforce.

- **Partnerships and Joint Ventures:**

  o **Collaboration with Saudi Aramco:** GE has entered joint ventures to develop energy solutions and support the oil and gas sector.

  o **Healthcare Initiatives:** Partnered with the Ministry of Health to modernize healthcare infrastructure and introduce advanced medical technologies.

- **Innovation and Research:**

  o **GE Saudi Innovation Center:** Opened in 2013 in Dhahran Techno Valley to foster innovation and collaboration with local institutions.

  o **Focus Areas:** Energy efficiency, digital industrial solutions, and sustainable technologies.

Success Factors

- **Alignment with Vision 2030:** GE's initiatives support the Kingdom's goals of economic diversification, localization, and technology transfer.

- **Cultural Integration:** Emphasis on understanding local culture and building relationships with key stakeholders.

- **Long-Term Commitment:** Demonstrated dedication through sustained investment and capacity building.

Case Study 2: Siemens

Background

Siemens, a global powerhouse in electrification, automation, and digitalization, has a significant footprint in Saudi Arabia, contributing to infrastructure development and industrial modernization.

Strategies and Outcomes

- **Local Manufacturing:**

  o Siemens Energy Hub: Established manufacturing facilities in Dammam for gas turbines and compressors.

  o Technology Transfer: Facilitated the transfer of advanced manufacturing technologies to the local workforce.

- **Human Capital Development:**

  o Training Programs: Implemented apprenticeship programs and technical education initiatives.

  o Employment Opportunities: Created jobs for Saudi nationals, promoting skills development in engineering and technology.

- **Digital Solutions:**

  o Smart Grid Projects: Collaborated with the Saudi Electricity Company to enhance grid reliability and efficiency.

  o Industry 4.0 Implementation: Supported Saudi industries in adopting automation and digitalization.

Success Factors

- **Strategic Partnerships:** Built strong relationships with government entities and local companies.

- **Adaptability:** Customized solutions to meet the specific needs of the Saudi market.

- **Sustainability Focus:** Aligned projects with environmental sustainability goals.

SUCCESSFUL STARTUPS

Case Study 3: Careem

Background

Careem, a ride-hailing company founded in 2012 in Dubai, expanded rapidly into Saudi Arabia, becoming a leading mobility platform in the region.

Strategies and Outcomes

- **Market Entry:**

  o **Localization:** Tailored services to meet local preferences, including features like cash payments and family-friendly options.

  o **Regulatory Compliance:** Worked closely with Saudi authorities to ensure adherence to local regulations.

- **Women Empowerment:**

  o **Female Drivers (Captains):** In 2018, following the lifting of the ban on women driving, Careem began recruiting female drivers, supporting women's economic participation.

  o **Safety Features:** Implemented safety measures to address cultural sensitivities and ensure passenger comfort.

- **Acquisition by Uber:**

  o Valuation: In 2019, Uber acquired Careem for $3.1 billion, marking one of the largest technology acquisitions in the Middle East.

  o Continued Operations: Careem continues to operate independently, expanding its services.

Success Factors

- **Understanding Local Needs:** Adapted services to align with cultural norms and consumer behavior.

- **Agility:** Responded quickly to regulatory changes and market opportunities.

- **Technology Integration:** Leveraged mobile technology to provide convenient and reliable services.

Case Study 4: Noon.com

Background

Noon.com is a Saudi-backed e-commerce platform launched in 2017 to serve the Middle East market, competing with global players like Amazon.

Strategies and Outcomes

- **Investment and Support:**

  o **Public Investment Fund (PIF):** The PIF provided significant funding, emphasizing the government's support for digital economy initiatives.

  o **Partnerships:** Collaborated with retailers and logistics providers to build a robust ecosystem.

- **Localization and Customer Experience:**

  o **Language and Currency:** Offered services in Arabic and local currencies.

  o **Product Range:** Curated a wide selection of products catering to regional preferences.

- **Expansion:**

  o **Market Presence:** Expanded operations to Egypt and the UAE.

  o **Service Diversification:** Introduced Noon Food and Noon Pay to broaden offerings.

Success Factors

- **Government Support:** Benefited from strategic investments aligning with Vision 2030's digital transformation goals.

- **Market Knowledge:** Deep understanding of local consumer behavior and market dynamics.

- **Infrastructure Investment:** Developed logistics and fulfillment centers to ensure efficient delivery.

Lessons Learned

Common Themes Across Success Stories

1. Alignment with National Goals:

   - Successful ventures often align with Saudi Arabia's Vision 2030 objectives, contributing to economic diversification, localization, and job creation.

2. Cultural Adaptation:

   - Understanding and respecting cultural norms is critical for market acceptance and building trust with consumers and partners.

3. Strategic Partnerships:

   - Collaborations with government entities, local businesses, and institutions facilitate market entry and expansion.

4. Investment in Human Capital:

   - Developing local talent through training and education programs enhances workforce capabilities and supports Saudization efforts.

5. Innovation and Technology:

   - Embracing digital transformation and innovative solutions positions companies for growth in an evolving market.

6. Regulatory Engagement:

   - Proactive engagement with regulatory bodies ensures compliance and can influence favorable policy developments.

Overcoming Challenges

- **Regulatory Changes:**

   o Companies must stay adaptable to navigate evolving regulations and policies.

- **Competition:**

   o Differentiation through unique value propositions and customer-centric approaches is essential.

- **Market Entry Barriers:**

   o Thorough market research and due diligence mitigate risks associated with entry barriers.

Potential Pitfalls and How to Avoid Them

1. Underestimating Cultural Nuances:

   - **Solution:** Invest in cultural training and hire local experts to bridge gaps.

2. Non-Compliance with Regulations:

   - **Solution:** Engage legal counsel familiar with Saudi laws and maintain open communication with authorities.

3. Insufficient Market Research:

   - **Solution:** Conduct a comprehensive market analysis to understand consumer behavior, competition, and demand.

4. Lack of Localization:

   - **Solution:** Adapt products and services to meet local needs and preferences.

5. Overlooking Saudization Requirements:

   - **Solution:** Develop strategic hiring plans to meet Saudization quotas and contribute to workforce development.

Emerging Opportunities Highlighted by Success Stories

- **Renewable Energy:**

   o With projects like the NEOM city focusing on sustainability, there's a growing demand for renewable energy solutions.

- **Entertainment and Tourism:**

  o The opening of the tourism sector presents opportunities in hospitality, cultural experiences, and leisure activities.

- **Healthcare and Biotechnology:**

  o The focus on healthcare modernization creates demand for medical technologies, pharmaceuticals, and biotech research.

- **FinTech and Digital Services:**

  o A young, tech-savvy population drives growth in digital banking, payments, and financial services.

CONCLUSION

The success stories highlighted in this chapter demonstrate that Saudi Arabia offers a fertile ground for investors who are willing to understand the market, adapt to cultural norms, and align their strategies with the Kingdom's vision for the future. By learning from these examples, investors can craft informed strategies that leverage the opportunities available while navigating potential challenges effectively.

VIA UNSPLASH ©

KEY TAKEAWAYS

- **Success Factors:**

  o Alignment with national objectives, cultural adaptation, strategic partnerships, and investment in innovation are critical for success.

- **Learning from Others:**

  o Analyzing successful cases provides actionable insights into market entry strategies and operational excellence.

- **Opportunity Recognition:**

  o Identifying sectors with government support and market demand enhances the potential for successful investment.

REFERENCES

- **General Electric (GE) Saudi Arabia:** www.ge.com/sa

- **Siemens Saudi Arabia:** www.siemens.com/sa

- **Careem: www.careem.com**

- **Noon.com: www.noon.com**

- **Vision 2030: www.vision2030.gov.sa**

- **Public Investment Fund (PIF):** www.pif.gov.sa

- **Ministry of Investment (MISA):** www.misa.gov.sa

RECOMMENDATIONS FOR INVESTORS

- **Conduct Thorough Research:**

  o Understand the specific dynamics of your target sector and how it fits within Saudi Arabia's economic landscape.

- **Engage with Local Stakeholders:**

  o Build relationships with government agencies, industry associations, and local businesses.

- **Invest in Localization:**

  o Tailor your products, services, and business practices to meet local needs and expectations.

- **Plan for the Long Term:**

  o Adopt a long-term perspective focused on sustainable growth and contribution to the local economy.

Chapter 9

Future Outlook

As Saudi Arabia continues its ambitious journey towards economic diversification and modernization under Vision 2030, the future presents a landscape of evolving opportunities and challenges. This chapter explores the economic forecasts for the Kingdom, identifies potential challenges and opportunities, and offers insights on how investors can adapt their strategies to align with the anticipated changes.

ECONOMIC FORECASTS PREDICTIONS FOR KEY SECTORS

Energy Sector

Oil and Gas

Sustained Importance: While global efforts toward decarbonization may affect long-term demand, oil and gas will remain significant to Saudi Arabia's economy in the foreseeable future.

Technological Advancements: Investments in carbon capture and storage (CCS) and enhanced oil recovery (EOR) technologies aim to make hydrocarbon extraction more efficient and environmentally friendly.

Global Market Position: Saudi Arabia is expected to maintain its role as a key player in OPEC+, influencing global oil supply and prices.

Renewable Energy

Growth Projections: The renewable energy sector is poised for exponential growth, with plans to generate 50% of the country's energy from renewable sources by 2030.

Investment Opportunities: Solar and wind energy projects, green hydrogen production, and energy storage solutions will attract significant investment.

Global Leadership in Green Hydrogen: Initiatives like the NEOM Green Hydrogen Project position Saudi Arabia to become a leading exporter of green hydrogen.

Technology and Innovation

Digital Economy Expansion: The digital sector's contribution to GDP is expected to increase significantly, driven by initiatives like the National Digital Transformation Program.

Artificial Intelligence (AI): The Kingdom aims to become a global leader in AI by 2030, with strategies to integrate AI across government services and industries.

Start-up Ecosystem Growth: Continued support for entrepreneurship will foster innovation, particularly in fintech, e-commerce, and biotechnology.

Tourism and Entertainment

Tourism Targets: Saudi Arabia aims to attract 100 million visitors annually by 2030, contributing 10% to GDP and creating one million jobs.

Mega-Projects Completion: Projects like NEOM, Qiddiya, and the Red Sea Development will redefine the tourism and entertainment landscape.

Cultural Exchange: Increased international tourism will enhance cultural understanding and global integration.

Healthcare and Biotechnology

Healthcare Modernization: Investments in healthcare infrastructure and services will improve quality and accessibility, with private sector participation playing a significant role.

Biotechnology Advancement: The establishment of research centers and partnerships will propel the biotechnology sector, focusing on pharmaceuticals and genetic research.

Mining and Industry

Mineral Exploration: Unlocking the Kingdom's estimated $1.3 trillion in mineral resources will diversify exports and industrial activities.

Industrial Growth: Expansion of manufacturing capabilities in sectors like automotive, defense, and electronics.

POTENTIAL CHALLENGES AND OPPORTUNITIES

Technological Disruption

Opportunities

Fourth Industrial Revolution (4IR): Adoption of 4IR technologies, such as the Internet of Things (IoT), robotics, and blockchain, will enhance productivity and create new business models.

Smart Cities Development: Projects like NEOM will serve as testbeds for integrating cutting-edge technologies into urban planning.

Challenges

Workforce Adaptation: The rapid pace of technological change requires upskilling and reskilling of the workforce to meet new job demands.

Cybersecurity Risks: Increased connectivity heightens vulnerability to cyber threats, necessitating robust security measures.

Environmental Sustainability Initiatives

Opportunities

Saudi Green Initiative: Commitment to environmental sustainability will open avenues in renewable energy, sustainable agriculture, and environmental technologies.

Carbon Circular Economy: Strategies to reduce, reuse, recycle, and remove carbon emissions will create investment opportunities in green technologies.

Challenges

Climate Change Impact: Addressing the effects of climate change, such as water scarcity and desertification, requires substantial investment and innovation.

Regulatory Compliance: Adhering to international environmental standards may increase operational costs in the short term.

Geopolitical Dynamics

Opportunities

Regional Integration: Strengthening ties with neighboring countries can enhance trade and investment flows.

Global Partnerships: Strategic alliances with global powers can facilitate technology transfer and market access.

Challenges

Regional Conflicts: Ongoing tensions in the Middle East may pose risks to stability and investor confidence.

Trade Policies: Global trade disputes and protectionism could impact export markets and supply chains.

Economic Diversification

Opportunities

Private Sector Growth: Privatization and deregulation efforts will open sectors previously dominated by the public sector to private investment.

SME Development: Support for small and medium-sized enterprises will stimulate innovation and job creation.

Challenges

Implementation Pace: The success of diversification hinges on the timely and effective implementation of reforms.

Fiscal Adjustments: Managing fiscal deficits and public debt levels while investing in diversification projects.

PREPARING FOR CHANGE

Adapting Investment Strategies

Sector Focus

Diversify Portfolio: Investors should consider a mix of traditional sectors like energy and emerging sectors such as technology, healthcare, and tourism.

Sustainability Alignment: Align investments with environmental sustainability initiatives to capitalize on government support and global trends.

Risk Management

Stay Informed: Regularly monitor economic indicators, policy developments, and geopolitical events.

Flexible Strategies: Be prepared to adjust investment plans in response to changing market conditions.

Embracing Innovation

Leverage Technology: Incorporate technological advancements to improve efficiency and competitiveness.

Invest in R&D: Support research and development to foster innovation and gain a competitive edge.

Human Capital Development

Talent Acquisition: Focus on recruiting and retaining skilled professionals who can drive growth and innovation.

Training Programs: Invest in employee development to build capabilities aligned with future industry needs.

Regulatory Compliance and Governance

Stay Updated on Reforms: Keep abreast of regulatory changes to ensure compliance and take advantage of new opportunities.

Corporate Governance: Strengthen governance structures to enhance transparency, accountability, and stakeholder confidence.

Cultural Adaptation

Cultural Intelligence: Deepen understanding of local customs and business practices to build stronger relationships.

Corporate Social Responsibility (CSR): Engage in CSR initiatives that contribute to social and environmental well-being.

Embracing the Future: Strategic Recommendations

Long-Term Vision

Align with Vision 2030: Develop strategies that support and benefit from the Kingdom's long-term goals.

Patience and Persistence: Recognize that substantial returns may require sustained commitment over time.

Partnerships and Collaboration

Local Partnerships: Collaborate with Saudi companies to leverage local knowledge and networks.

Public-Private Partnerships (PPPs): Participate in PPPs to engage in large-scale projects with government support.

Innovation and Entrepreneurship

Support Startups: Invest in the startup ecosystem to foster innovation and gain early access to emerging technologies.

Adapt Business Models: Be open to evolving traditional business models to meet future market demands.

CONCLUSION

The future of investing in Saudi Arabia is marked by significant transformation and potential. The Kingdom's commitment to diversification, technological advancement, and sustainable development creates a dynamic environment ripe with opportunities. However, navigating this landscape requires strategic foresight, adaptability, and a deep understanding of the evolving economic and cultural context.

By aligning investment strategies with the Kingdom's vision, embracing innovation, and proactively managing risks, investors can position themselves to capitalize on Saudi Arabia's growth trajectory. The journey ahead promises to be both challenging and rewarding, offering a chance to be part of one of the most ambitious economic transformations of our time.

KEY TAKEAWAYS

- **Growth Prospects:** Key sectors like renewable energy, technology, and tourism are expected to drive economic growth.

- **Opportunity Amidst Change:** Technological disruption and sustainability initiatives present both challenges and opportunities for savvy investors.

- **Strategic Adaptation:** Investors must adapt their strategies to align with future trends, regulatory changes, and market dynamics.

- **Long-Term Commitment:** Success in Saudi Arabia's evolving market requires patience, resilience, and a long-term perspective.

REFERENCES

- Vision 2030: www.vision2030.gov.sa
- Ministry of Investment (MISA): www.misa.gov.sa
- Saudi Green Initiative: www.saudigreeninitiative.org
- National Digital Transformation Program: ndu.gov.sa
- International Monetary Fund (IMF) Reports: www.imf.org
- World Bank Group: www.worldbank.org
- Saudi Central Bank (SAMA): www.sama.gov.sa

Conclusion

Throughout this book, we have explored the rich tapestry of opportunities and considerations that define the investment landscape in Saudi Arabia. Here are the key insights gleaned from our journey:

RECAP OF KEY INSIGHTS

Throughout this book, we have explored the rich tapestry of opportunities and considerations that define the investment landscape in Saudi Arabia. Here are the key insights gleaned from our journey:

1. **Dynamic Economic Transformation:** Saudi Arabia is undergoing a significant transformation under Vision 2030, aiming to diversify its economy away from oil dependency and foster sustainable growth across various sectors.

2. **Favorable Legal and Regulatory Environment:** The Kingdom has implemented progressive reforms to attract foreign investment, including allowing 100% foreign ownership in many sectors, streamlining business setup processes, and enhancing investor protections.

3. **Strategic Investment Opportunities:**

   • **Energy Sector:** Ambitious renewable energy initiatives, such as the Saudi Green Initiative, offer substantial opportunities in solar, wind, and green hydrogen projects.

   • **Infrastructure and Mega-Projects:** Projects like NEOM, The Red Sea Development, and Qiddiya present vast opportunities in construction, technology integration, and sustainable development.

   • **Technology and Innovation:** Government support for digital transformation and a growing start-up ecosystem create a fertile ground for investments in technology and innovation.

   • **Healthcare and Education:** Privatization efforts and modernization initiatives in these sectors open doors for investment in healthcare services, medical tourism, and educational institutions.

   • **Tourism and Entertainment:** The opening of the tourism sector and cultural projects offer opportunities in hospitality, entertainment, and cultural exchange.

4. **Navigating Cultural Nuances:** Understanding and respecting Saudi cultural norms, business etiquette, and social customs is crucial for building strong relationships and successful partnerships.

5. **Risk Management and Compliance:** Identifying potential risks—political, economic, legal, and compliance-related—is essential. Implementing robust risk mitigation strategies ensures the safeguarding of investments.

6. **Practical Steps to Investing:** A clear roadmap for market entry strategies, business setup procedures, understanding labor laws, and navigating banking and financial services is vital for establishing operations effectively.

7. **Learning from Success Stories:** Case studies of multinational corporations and successful start-ups illustrate the importance of aligning with national goals, adapting to cultural expectations, investing in local talent, and embracing innovation.

8. **Future Outlook:** Economic forecasts indicate promising growth in key sectors. Technological advancements and sustainability initiatives present both opportunities and challenges, requiring investors to adapt their strategies accordingly.

FINAL THOUGHTS ON INVESTING IN SAUDI ARABIA

Investing in Saudi Arabia offers a unique convergence of tradition and modernity, where ancient cultural heritage meets ambitious visions for the future. The Kingdom's strategic initiatives, robust economic reforms, and commitment to creating a business-friendly environment make it a compelling destination for investors seeking growth and diversification.

The nation's young and dynamic population, coupled with significant government investment in education and technology, positions Saudi Arabia as a hub for innovation and entrepreneurship. The emphasis on sustainability and renewable energy aligns with global trends, offering avenues for investors interested in contributing to a greener future.

However, success in the Saudi market is not without challenges. It requires a nuanced understanding of the local culture, legal landscape, and regulatory requirements. Patience, adaptability, and a long-term perspective are essential attributes for investors aiming to establish a lasting presence.

By embracing the country's vision and aligning investment strategies with national objectives, investors can play a meaningful role in Saudi Arabia's transformative journey. The Kingdom's openness to foreign investment, combined with its strategic location and economic potential, creates a landscape ripe with possibilities.

Encouragement for Investors

As we stand at the cusp of a new era in Saudi Arabia's economic development, the opportunities for investors are both abundant and diverse. The nation's commitment to progress and modernization presents a welcoming environment for those ready to contribute to and benefit from this transformative period.

For the Aspiring Investor:

- **Seize the Moment:** The proactive reforms and initiatives underway make this an opportune time to enter the Saudi market.

- **Be a Pioneer:** Join the ranks of forward-thinking businesses that are shaping the future of industries in the Kingdom.

- **Make an Impact:** Beyond financial returns, your investment can contribute to societal advancement, job creation, and the realization of sustainable development goals.

Your Path Forward:

- **Educate and Prepare:** Leverage the insights provided in this book to inform your strategies and decisions.
- **Engage Locally:** Build relationships with local partners, authorities, and communities to enhance your understanding and integration.
- **Adapt and Innovate:** Be ready to adapt to changing circumstances and embrace innovation as a driver of success.

Embrace the Opportunity:

Saudi Arabia's doors are open to investors who share its vision for a prosperous and diversified economy. By approaching this market with respect, diligence, and enthusiasm, you position yourself not only for potential financial success but also for contributing to a historic period of growth and transformation.

Final Encouragement:

Embarking on an investment journey in Saudi Arabia is more than a business decision; it's an invitation to participate in a nation's ambitious pursuit of progress. The road may present challenges, but the rewards—both tangible and intangible—promise to be significant.

Take the leap with confidence, armed with knowledge and inspired by possibility. The Kingdom of Saudi Arabia awaits those ready to invest in its future and, in doing so, shape their own.

Thank you for joining us on this exploration of investing in Saudi Arabia. May your ventures be successful and your contributions meaningful in this land of opportunity.

Appendices

Resource Directory

A comprehensive list of key government agencies, investment forums, and associations that can provide valuable support and information for investors in Saudi Arabia. This resource directory serves as a starting point for investors to connect with key institutions that can provide assistance, information, and networking opportunities essential for successful investment in Saudi Arabia. Engaging with these agencies and organizations can offer valuable insights into the business environment, regulatory landscape, and potential partnerships.

Government Agencies

1. Ministry of Investment (MISA)

   - **Website:** www.misa.gov.sa

   - **Overview:** Facilitates foreign investment, providing licensing services, investment opportunities, and investor support.

2. Ministry of Commerce

   - **Website:** www.mc.gov.sa

   - **Overview:** Oversees commercial and investment activities, including company registration and commercial laws.

3. Ministry of Finance

   - **Website:** www.mof.gov.sa

   - **Overview:** Responsible for fiscal policies, budgeting, and economic planning.

4. Saudi Central Bank (SAMA)

   - **Website:** www.sama.gov.sa

   - **Overview:** Regulates the banking sector, monetary policy, and ensures financial stability.

5. Capital Market Authority (CMA)

   - **Website:** www.cma.org.sa

   - **Overview:** Regulates capital markets, including securities, mutual funds, and investor protection.

6. Zakat, Tax and Customs Authority (ZATCA)

   - **Website:** www.zatca.gov.sa

   - **Overview:** Manages taxation, including corporate tax, VAT, and customs regulations.

7. General Authority for Statistics (GaStat)

   - **Website:** www.stats.gov.sa

   - **Overview:** Provides official statistical data on economic, social, and demographic indicators.

8. Ministry of Human Resources and Social Development (MHRSD)

   - **Website:** www.hrsd.gov.sa

   - **Overview:** Manages labor laws, Saudization policies, and workforce development.

9. General Organization for Social Insurance (GOSI)

- **Website:** www.gosi.gov.sa

- **Overview:** Administers social insurance programs, including pensions and workplace injury compensation.

10. Saudi Customs

- **Website:** www.customs.gov.sa

- **Overview:** Oversees import and export regulations and customs procedures.

11. Saudi Authority for Industrial Cities and Technology Zones (MODON)

- **Website:** www.modon.gov.sa

- **Overview:** Develops and manages industrial cities and technology zones, providing infrastructure and services.

12. Saudi Industrial Development Fund (SIDF)

- **Website:** www.sidf.gov.sa

- **Overview:** Offers financing for industrial projects to support economic diversification.

13. Public Investment Fund (PIF)

- **Website:** www.pif.gov.sa

- **Overview:** The sovereign wealth fund investing in strategic sectors domestically and internationally.

14. National Center for Privatization & PPP (NCP)

- **Website:** www.ncp.gov.sa

- **Overview:** Facilitates privatization programs and public-private partnerships.

15. General Authority for Competition (GAC)

- **Website:** www.gac.gov.sa

- **Overview:** Promotes fair competition and combats monopolistic practices.

16. Saudi Export Development Authority (SAUDI EXPORTS)

- **Website:** www.saudiexports.sa

- **Overview:** Supports exporters and promotes Saudi products in international markets.

17. Saudi Food and Drug Authority (SFDA)

- **Website:** www.sfda.gov.sa

- **Overview:** Regulates food, drugs, medical devices, and cosmetics to ensure safety and quality.

18. Saudi Standards, Metrology and Quality Organization (SASO)

- **Website:** www.saso.gov.sa

- **Overview:** Sets standards and specifications for products and services to ensure quality and safety.

19. Saudi Center for Commercial Arbitration (SCCA)

- **Website:** www.sadr.org

- **Overview:** Provides arbitration and mediation services for commercial disputes.

20. Monsha'at (Small and Medium Enterprises General Authority)

- **Website:** www.monshaat.gov.sa

- **Overview:** Supports SMEs through funding, training, and policy advocacy.

Investment Forums and Associations

1. Council of Saudi Chambers

   - **Website:** www.csc.org.sa
   - **Overview:** Represents the private sector and facilitates communication between businesses and government.

2. Riyadh Chamber of Commerce and Industry

   - **Website:** www.riyadhchamber.sa
   - **Overview:** Provides services and support to businesses in the Riyadh region.

3. Jeddah Chamber of Commerce and Industry

   - **Website:** www.jcci.org.sa
   - **Overview:** Supports businesses in Jeddah, offering networking opportunities and resources.

4. Eastern Province Chamber of Commerce and Industry

   - **Website:** www.chamber.org.sa
   - **Overview:** Serves businesses in the Eastern Province, facilitating trade and investment.

5. Saudi British Joint Business Council (SBJBC)

   - **Website:** www.sbjbc.org
   - **Overview:** Promotes trade and investment between Saudi Arabia and the United Kingdom.

6. U.S.-Saudi Arabian Business Council (USS-ABC)

   - **Website:** www.us-sabc.org
   - **Overview:** Enhances trade and investment relations between the United States and Saudi Arabia.

7. Saudi-Italian Business Council

   - **Contact:** Through the Council of Saudi Chambers
   - **Overview:** Facilitates business cooperation between Saudi Arabia and Italy.

8. Saudi German Business Dialogue

   - **Contact:** Via the German-Saudi Arabian Liaison Office for Economic Affairs (GESALO)
   - **Website:** saudiarabien.ahk.de
   - **Overview:** Promotes bilateral trade and investment between Saudi Arabia and Germany.

9. MENA Investment Congress

   - **Website:** Event-specific; check with MISA or local chambers for details.
   - **Overview:** An annual event that brings together investors and businesses in the Middle East and North Africa region.

10. Gulf Cooperation Council (GCC) Chambers

    - **Website:** www.fgccc.org
    - **Overview:** Facilitates cooperation among GCC countries' chambers of commerce.

11. Saudi International Exhibition and Convention Center

- **Website:** www.recexpo.com

- **Overview:** Provides information on conferences and exhibitions in Saudi Arabia.

12. Invest Saudi

- **Website:** www.investsaudi.sa

- **Overview:** An initiative by MISA to promote investment opportunities and provide investor support.

13. Saudi Venture Capital Company (SVC)

- **Website:** www.svc.com.sa

- **Overview:** Supports startups and SMEs through venture capital and private equity investments.

14. KAUST Innovation

- **Website:** innovation.kaust.edu.sa

- **Overview:** The innovation and economic development arm of King Abdullah University of Science and Technology, promoting research and startups.

15. MISK Foundation

- **Website:** www.misk.org.sa

- **Overview:** A non-profit organization dedicated to empowering youth in education, entrepreneurship, and technology.

16. Saudi Arabian General Investment Authority (SAGIA)

Note: Now integrated into MISA.

17. Saudi Stock Exchange (Tadawul)

- **Website:** www.saudiexchange.sa

- **Overview:** The sole entity authorized to act as a securities exchange in Saudi Arabia, providing access to capital markets.

18. Saudi Industrial Property Authority (MODON)

- **Website:** www.modon.gov.sa

- **Overview:** Develops and manages industrial cities and technology zones, offering opportunities for industrial investment.

19. Entrepreneurship Vision 2030

- **Contact:** Via Monsha'at or MISA

- **Overview:** An initiative to promote entrepreneurship in line with Vision 2030 objectives.

20. Saudi Chambers International Roadshows and Events

- **Overview:** Regular events organized domestically and internationally to promote investment opportunities.

- **Contact:** Check with local chambers or MISA for upcoming events.

Note: Contact details such as phone numbers and email addresses can be obtained from the respective websites. It is advisable to verify the currentness of the information, as websites and organizational structures may change over time.

About the Author

Mohammad Bahareth is a Saudi author, motivational speaker, and business consultant whose journey challenges stereotypes and redefines possibility. Living with dyslexia and ADHD, Mohammad turned what many see as obstacles into the driving force behind his creativity, resilience, and original thinking.

With more than 50 published works in English and Arabic—including the acclaimed Sherlock Holmes 2012 series—Mohammad is a prolific storyteller known for blending imagination with insight. His work spans fiction, strategy, and social advocacy, earning him recognition across literary and professional spheres.

A member of the Forbes Business Council and a contributor to Inc. Arabia, Mohammad has led over 42,000 consultations in 16 countries, guiding organizations of all sizes toward strategic growth and innovation. His proprietary models—The Bahareth Method and Goal Model Canvas—help turn bold ideas into measurable impact.

Passionate about inclusion, he founded the Mohammad Bahareth Charity, where his Dyslexia Awareness Initiative has influenced national policy and empowered countless lives. His mission: to uncover the next generation of changemakers hidden in plain sight.

Currently, Mohammad is working on two ambitious novels: Paws of Destiny, a tale of genetically evolved cats shaping human history, and OctoPlanet, a profound reflection on identity and perception. His fiction is as daring as his life—unafraid to question norms and celebrate difference.

Through books, talks, and ventures, Mohammad lives by his signature theme: "Experience of Uniqueness." Whether on stage or on the page, his voice invites others to embrace their individuality, think differently, and leave a mark that matters.

**Unlock more insights and offerings
from Mohammad Bahareth.**

Scan the QR Code now to visit the official store:

www.ingramcontent.com/pod-product-compliance
Lightning Source LLC
Chambersburg PA
CBHW082111210326
41599CB00033B/6669